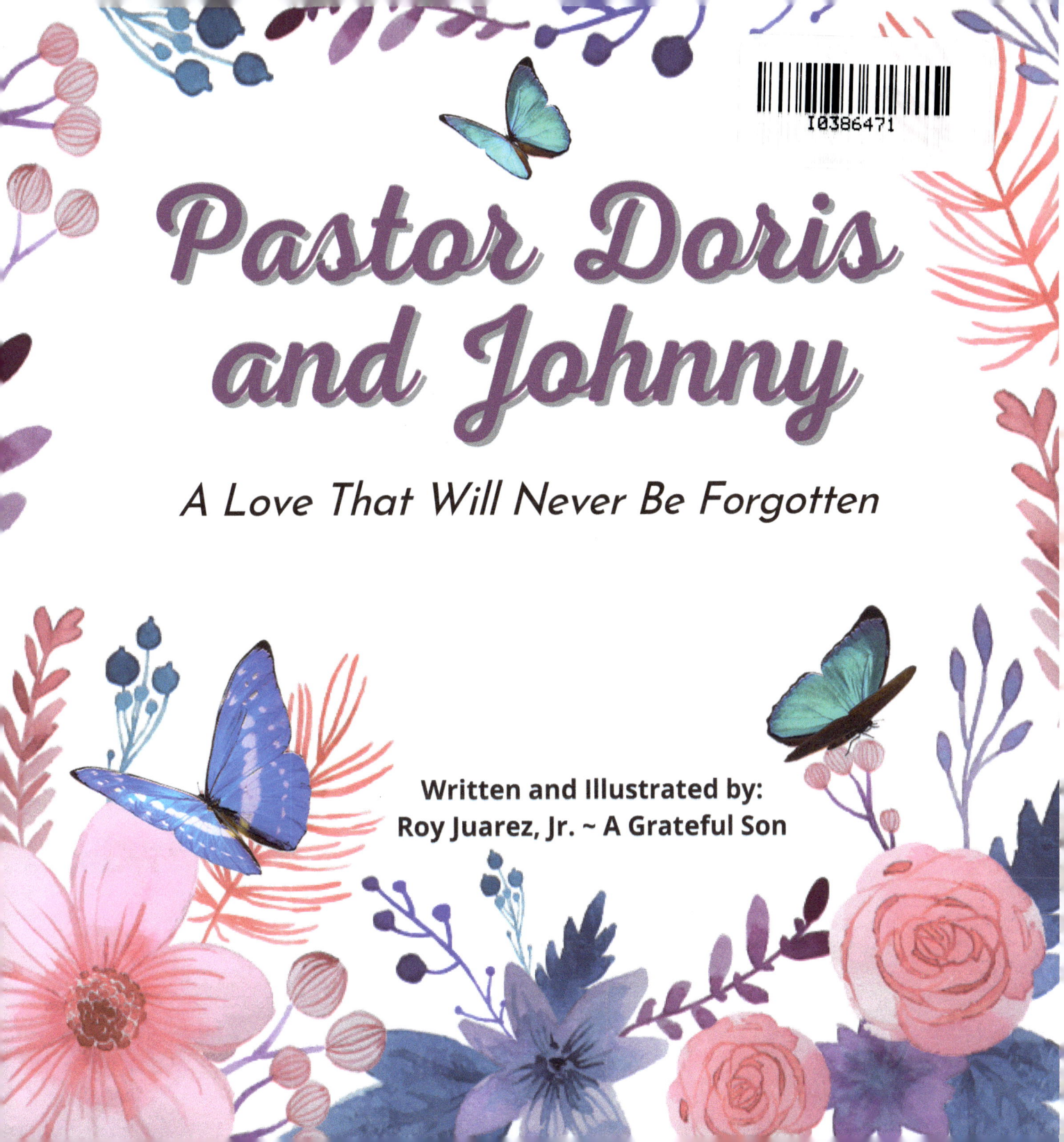

This Book Belongs to:

_____

But they that wait upon the LORD shall renew their strength; they shall mount up with wings as eagles; they shall run, and not be weary; and they shall walk, and not faint.

Isaiah 40:31 KJV

Johnny and I met many years ago at a public pool.

We started dating and fell in love.

Johnny asked me to marry him and I said, yes!

I tried to drive his new car and crashed it into a tree.

There was one tree in the whole yard and she found it.

He loved me and we got married anyway.

We shared so many good times together.
Some tough times but our love pulled us through.

We had three beautiful children.

Our brave son John,

our strong daughter Lisa,

and our kind Cindy.

We had one more son but I will tell you about him later.

My husband Johnny is so brave. He was a firefighter and helped so many people.

I like helping people too.

I created a nonprofit called, Offerings of Peace Ministries to help women and children.

I held home meetings to get started.

We eventually turned the organization into a church and welcomed everyone!

Our son grew up and joined the fire department like his dad.

Our daughter Lisa joined the church choir and helped in the kitchen to feed the congregation.

Our kind Cindy always made everyone laugh and feel welcomed.

One evening, before service, a young boy named Roy was waiting for me outside the church with his little brother Ray.

He asked, "Pastor Doris can we live in your church?
We promise to clean it for you."

I looked at him and said, "No, you will live with Pastor Johnny and Me."

We opened our home, and our children opened their hearts.

Soon after, our grandchildren and Roy's little sister moved in!

Deriene, Danielle, Samantha, and Tiffany built so many good memories together.

One evening, Roy's older sister Amy came to spend the night and she never left! It's okay, we loved her too!

Roy lived with us for four years before graduating high school and going on to college.

GOD taught US...

how to Forgive

and have COMPASSION

but what we are most grateful for is...

the huge family He gave us. One we will always cherish.

Guess what? The Lord has great things for you too.

Always be there for each other and remember, we will always love you. - Pastor Doris and Johnny

About the Author

Pastor Johnny, Roy, Pastor Doris, and Baby Ray

Roy Juarez, Jr. is an international motivational speaker, author, and entrepreneur who has spent his entire career inspiring students, parents, and educators.

In 2005, Juarez began his journey as an activist for at-risk youth and families. He founded IMPACTtruth, Inc., a human development company. Today, that company has grown into a team of powerhouse speakers and workshop presenters globally fighting social injustices.

As a children's book author, Juarez aims to introduce core values, practical life lessons, and joy into his young readers' lives.

Pastor Doris and Johnny – A Love That Will Never Be Forgotten is his gift to his adoptive parents, who helped shape and molded him into the man he is today.

Pastor Doris and Johnny
A Love That Will Never Be Forgotten
Copyright© 2021 by IMPACTpublishing, Inc.

www.ImpactPublishing.Ink

All rights reserved. This book or any portion thereof may not be reproduced or used in any manner whatsoever without the express written permission of the publisher.

Printed in the United States.

First Edition, 2021

ISBN: 978-1-955509-00-8

Impact Publishing, Inc.
P.O. Box 27311
San Antonio, TX 78227

Graphic Design by: Indalecio Chavez, Jr.
Formatted by: John Rey Lim

www.ingramcontent.com/pod-product-compliance
Lightning Source LLC
Chambersburg PA
CBHW061105070526
44579CB00011B/148